I SPY with my little eye, something beginning with...

A is for

Alligator

I SPY with my little eye, something beginning with...

B

B is for

Bat

I SPY with my little eye, something beginning with...

C and D

C is for
Cat

D is for
Dog

I SPY with my little eye, something beginning with...

E is for

Elephant

I SPY with my little eye, something beginning with...

F

F is for

Frog

I SPY with my little eye, something beginning with...

G and H

G is for

H is for

Giraffe   Horse

I SPY with my little eye, something beginning with...

I is for

Iguana

I SPY with my little eye, something beginning with...

J

J is for

Jellyfish

I SPY with my little eye, something beginning with...

K

K is for

Kangaroo

I SPY with my little eye, something beginning with...

L and M

I SPY with my little eye, something beginning with...

N

N is for

Narwhal

I SPY with my little eye, something beginning with...

O is for

Owl

I SPY with my little eye, something beginning with...

P and Q

Q is for
Quail

P is for
Panda

I SPY with my little eye, something beginning with...

R

R is for Raccoon

I SPY with my little eye, something beginning with...

S is for

Snake

I SPY with my little eye, something beginning with...

T

T is for

Turtle

I SPY with my little eye, something beginning with...

U

U is for

Unicorn

I SPY with my little eye, something beginning with...

V

V is for

Viperfish

I SPY with my little eye, something beginning with...

W

W is for

Whale

I SPY with my little eye, something beginning with...

X

X is for

Xerus

I SPY with my little eye,
something beginning with...

Y

Y is for

Yak

I SPY with my little eye, something beginning with...

Z